STARS of WORLD TENNIS

By Tyler Blue

Abbeville Kids
An Imprint of Abbeville Press
New York London

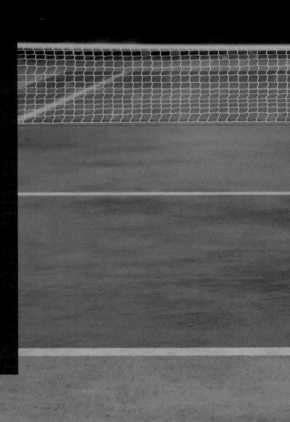

Statistics are current as of February 5, 2024.

Project editor: Lauren Orthey
Copy editor: Ashley Benning
Designer: Ada Rodriguez
Production director: Louise Kurtz

PHOTOGRAPHY CREDITS

Adobe Stock: front cover background (Yash); pp. 2–3 (Delcio F/peopleimages.com); pp. 4–5 (LeArchitecto)

Flickr: pp. 62–63 (Daniel Cooper)

Icon Sportswire: front cover left and right (Ian Johnson); p. 7 and back cover top left (John Cordes); p. 9 (Shelley Lipton); p. 11 (Speed Media); p. 13 (David Saffran); p. 15 (Chaz Niell); p. 17 (Speed Media); p. 19 (Jason Heidrich); p. 21 (Chaz Niell); p. 23 (John Cordes); pp. 25, 27 (Jason Heidrich); p. 31 (Antoine Couvercelle); p. 33 (Speed Media); p. 35 (John Cordes); p. 37 and back cover bottom left (Jason Heidrich); p. 39 (Michele Eve Sandberg); pp. 41, 43, 45, 47 (Jason Heidrich); p. 49 (Julian Avram); p. 51 (Antoine Couvercelle); p. 53 (Jason Heidrich); pp. 55, 57 (JB Autissier/Panoramic); p. 59 and back cover right (Julian Avram); p. 61 (David John Griffin)

Wikimedia Commons: p. 29 (Charlie Cowins)

First edition
10 9 8 7 6 5 4 3 2 1

Library of Congress Cataloging-in-Publication Data
Names: Blue, Tyler, author.
Title: Stars of World Tennis / Tyler Blue.
Description: First edition. | New York, N.Y. : Abbeville Kids, [2024] |
    Series: Abbeville sports | Audience: Ages 8–12 | Audience: Grades 2–3 |
    Summary: "Profiles of twenty-eight of today's top men's and women's
    tennis players"–Provided by publisher.
Identifiers: LCCN 2024013247 | ISBN 9780789215000 (hardcover)
Subjects: LCSH: Tennis players–Biography–Juvenile literature. | Women
    tennis players–Biography–Juvenile literature.
Classification: LCC GV994.A1 B | DDC 796.342092/2 [B]–dc23/eng/20240411
LC record available at https://lccn.loc.gov/2024013247

For bulk and premium sales and for text adoption procedures, write to Customer Service Manager, Abbeville Press, 655 Third Avenue, New York, NY 10017, or call 1-800-Artbook.

Visit Abbeville Kids online at www.abbeillefamily.com.

CONTENTS

Carlos Alcaraz

Spain's Carlos Alcaraz made history when, at the age of 19, he finished the 2022 Association of Tennis Professionals season ranked as the No. 1 tennis player in the world. Nobody that young had ever accomplished such a feat. The biggest shock, however, might have been that Alcaraz's meteoric rise to the summit of the tennis world actually was no surprise at all.

The story begins two generations ago in El Palmar, a small village in southeastern Spain, when Alcaraz's grandfather—Carlos Alcaraz Lerma—helped establish tennis courts at a local hunting club. The eldest Carlos passed his love for tennis down to his son—Carlos Sr.—who competed at a high level within Spain before becoming a tennis coach.

There was never a doubt, then, that Carlos Sr.'s son—widely known as Carlitos—would be introduced to the game at an early age. But nobody could have foreseen his prodigious talent. By the time he was four, members of the club already were in awe of the young boy's game and predicted Carlitos would be a champion one day.

Breaking into the upper echelons of tennis requires more than talent, though. Traveling around the world to tournaments requires money—more money than the six-member Alcaraz family could spare. Luckily, one of those impressed club members was Alfonso López Rueda, the tennis-crazed president of a Spanish dessert and candy company. López Rueda agreed to sponsor Alcaraz, giving him the resources he needed to compete at the highest levels.

Alcaraz proved to be a wise investment. He shot up the ranks with a creative, dynamic all-court style of play that stood out at a time when the game seemed to be all about using baseline rallies to wear down your opponent. In contrast, Alcaraz liked to smother his opponents with drop shots and constantly looked for opportunities to approach the net. He has credited the variety in his game to his father, who taught him the correct technique for every shot.

In 2022, Alcaraz was a revelation. At the Madrid Open that year, he beat legends Rafael Nadal and Novak Djokovic in the quarterfinals and semifinals, respectively, on his way to the championship. He won his first Grand Slam title later that year by defeating Casper Ruud of Norway in four sets in the U.S. Open. The next year, he won his second major, this time at Wimbledon, while reaching the semifinals of both the French and U.S. Opens.

He couldn't hold on to his No. 1 ranking, however. The 20-year-old Spaniard with two Grand Slam championships already under his belt ended 2023 at No. 2, behind the great Djokovic. Don't bet on him staying there for long.

Born: **May 5, 2003**
Hometown: **El Palmar, Spain**
Height: **6'**
Plays: **Right**
Turned pro: **2018**
Career best ranking (singles):
    1 (Sept. 12, 2022)
Grand Slam titles: **2**

Ashleigh Barty

On March 22, 2022, Ashleigh Barty was the undisputed queen of women's professional tennis. The 25-year-old had just captured her third Grand Slam title two months earlier, becoming the first Australian to win the Australian Open in 42 years. She was entering her 114th straight week of being the No. 1 ranked women's player. Then, on March 23, Barty announced her retirement.

While the news sent shock waves across the world of tennis, anyone who knew Barty or had followed her career shouldn't have been very surprised. After all, it was not the first time the talented superstar had walked away from the sport she made look so easy.

Barty, a native of Ipswich, Australia, was just four years old when she found an old squash racket and began hitting balls against the garage wall for hours. Her father Robert, a member of the Ngaragu Aboriginal group and former amateur golf champion, called Jim Joyce, the coach at the West Brisbane Tennis Centre. Joyce told Robert he didn't start coaching children until they turned eight. But when he saw Ashleigh's hand-eye coordination and focus firsthand, he quickly decided to make an exception.

Because Ashleigh was on the small side, Joyce devised a playing style for her that was varied and creative. Under his tutelage, her game took off. In June 2011, she won the Junior Wimbledon championship, but the grind was starting to get to her. Tired of all the time spent away from home and overwhelmed by the attention, Barty fell into a depression, and in September 2014 she decided to take a hiatus.

Though no longer subject to the rigors of the professional tennis circuit, Barty by no means stayed idle. Remarkably, she quickly took up another sport, signing with a professional cricket team in Brisbane. She had no experience with the sport, but apparently her ability to smash balls with sticks was not confined to tennis. The bonds she made with other girls around her age in a team setting reinvigorated Barty, and after hitting some tennis balls one day with former doubles partner Casey Dellacqua, she decided it was time to return to tennis.

So in 2016 Barty came back. And she won her first Women's Tennis Association title in 2017. Two years later, she won her first Grand Slam at the French Open and rose to No. 1 in the world a couple of weeks later after winning the Birmingham Classic. She remained a dominant figure, coming back from a COVID-19-induced break to win Wimbledon in 2021.

In a sport that has in recent years seen its fair share of ageless wonders—Serena and Venus Williams competed into their 40s, as did Roger Federer—Barty's decision to hang up her racket just as she reached her prime is a rarity. Now, more than two years into retirement, Barty, who welcomed her first child into the world in the summer of 2023, doesn't sound like she has any regrets. Asked once why she retired, Barty simply replied, "I achieved my dreams."

Born: **Apr. 24, 1996**
Hometown: **Ipswich, Australia**
Height: **5'5"**
Plays: **Right**
Turned pro: **2010**
Career best ranking (singles): **1**
  (June 24, 2019)
Grand Slam titles: **3**

Marin Čilić

When Zdenko Čilić was a teenager growing up in the small town of Međjugorje in Bosnia-Herzegovina, his uncle wanted to take him to Croatia to pursue an education and play soccer. However, Zdenko's father nixed the idea. He needed Zdenko to work the family's tobacco fields and vineyards.

Zdenko's athletic dreams died then and there, but the experience had a profound impact on him. Should he ever have children, he would do everything in his power to encourage their dreams and give them the opportunities he never had. So, years later, when his seven-year-old son Marin first showed an interest in tennis, Zdenko noted the inadequacy of the town's tennis facilities and decided to build a court in his backyard.

And when Marin had an opportunity to train in Zagreb, where the Croatian federation's training center is located, the 14-year-old had the complete support of his parents. The move to a bigger city several hours away from his family was difficult on Marin, but he recognized the sacrifice his parents were making for him and was determined to seize this opportunity.

In Zagreb, Marin caught the eye of Goran Ivanišević, a former Wimbledon champion and Croatian hero. With Ivanišević's help and guidance, Čilić eventually moved to Italy, where he trained with Australian coach Bob Brett. Under Brett's tutelage, Čilić—who by this time had grown to a height of 6'6"—turned pro in 2005 at the age of 17 and was sniffing the top 20 by the end of 2008.

Čilić's game is built around a killer serve and a flat, stinging forehand. Even so, the sport at that time was dominated by a small group of standouts—Roger Federer, Rafael Nadal, Novak Djokovic, and Andy Murray—and Čilić struggled to make inroads. Entering 2014, he had a 2–22 record against that quartet.

Then came the 2014 U.S. Open. Čilić played well enough to make the semifinals, where Federer awaited. Federer had won all five previous matches between the two, but on that night, Čilić played a nearly flawless match and won in straight sets. He then defeated Japan's Kei Nishikori in the championship. Finally, Čilić was on top of the tennis world.

From the 2005 French Open through the 2020 French Open, a mere seven men took all 61 Grand Slam tournaments—and Čilić was one of them. After his U.S. Open title, he returned to Međjugorje, a town of about 3,000. Tens of thousands of people showed up to cheer their local hero. His journey was long and arduous, but in the end a success.

And it all started with an opportunity.

Born: **Sept. 28, 1988**
Hometown: **Međjugorje, Bosnia and Herzegovina**
Height: **6'6"**
Plays: **Right**
Turned pro: **2005**
Career best ranking (singles): **3 (Jan. 29, 2018)**
Grand Slam titles: **1**

Kim Clijsters

Former world No. 1 Kim Clijsters of Belgium entered the 2009 U.S. Open as an unranked wild card. In May 2007, exhausted from dealing with injuries and wanting to start a family, Clijsters had stunned the tennis world by announcing her retirement at age 23. By March 2009, though, the new mother had decided to make a comeback.

The U.S. Open would mark just her third tournament since returning to the game. Suffice it to say that not a lot was expected of her. But with her 18-month-old daughter Jada by her side, Clijsters played like it was 2005 when she won the tournament. She cruised into the semifinals where she beat Serena Williams. Then she dispatched Caroline Wozniacki in the finals, becoming just the third mother—and the first since Evonne Goolagong won Wimbledon in 1980—to take a Grand Slam title.

Clijsters definitely had the pedigree of a champion. Her father Leo played professional soccer and was named Belgium's Player of the Year in 1988. Her mother Els was a Belgian national junior gymnastics champion before back issues shortened her career. Kim was lucky to inherit her father's power and perseverance and her mother's flexibility.

Once, when Kim was five, she stayed with her uncle and cousins while her mom went with her dad on a soccer-related trip. She tagged along to one of her relative's tennis lessons, standing on the sidelines, chasing after balls—and falling in love. When her parents returned, Kim told them she wanted to play tennis, and they found a place for her to begin lessons.

By 11, Kim was the Belgian junior champion, and she started appearing on the Women's Tennis Association tour in 1999. In 2003, she briefly rose to a No. 1 world ranking, finishing that year ranked No. 2. She became a fixture in Grand Slam finals, making four appearances from 2001 to 2004, but losing each time. Finally, in the 2005 U.S. Open, Clijsters had her big breakthrough, defeating Venus Williams, Maria Sharapova, and Mary Pierce in consecutive rounds to claim her first Grand Slam title.

Just two years after that triumph, dealing with ankle and wrist injuries and about to get married, Clijsters stepped away from professional tennis. Then, in 2009, Tim Henman asked Clijsters to play an exhibition match with him against Steffi Graf and Andre Agassi under the new Wimbledon roof. Not wanting to embarrass herself, Clijsters started to train, which got her competitive juices flowing again. Before long, she was itching to return for real.

Clijsters successfully defended her surprising 2009 U.S. Open victory by winning the tournament for a third time in 2010. She followed that up with an Australian Open championship in 2011. Once more, she found herself ranked No. 1 in the world—the first time a mom had reached that height. Clijsters retired for a second time in 2012 before attempting another comeback in 2020 that was derailed in part by the global pandemic. The four-time Grand Slam champion retired for good in 2022.

Born: **June 8, 1983**

Hometown: **Bilzen, Belgium**

Height: **5'8"**

Plays: **Right**

Turned pro: **1997**

Career best ranking:

Singles: **1 (Aug. 11, 2003)**

Doubles: **1 (Aug. 4, 2003)**

Grand Slam titles: **4**

Juan Martín del Potro

In the 2009 U.S. Open, Argentinian Juan Martín del Potro pulled off an unprecedented feat. The then 20-year-old defeated third-seeded Rafael Nadal in the semifinals before vanquishing world No. 1 Roger Federer the very next day in a five-set thriller to capture his first Grand Slam title. Before then, nobody had beaten Nadal and Federer in the same Grand Slam tournament, and del Potro seemed poised to be the one to finally break their stranglehold on the sport.

Unfortunately, not all stories have a happy ending.

Del Potro hails from Tandil, a city of about 150,000 people that lies some 250 miles south of Buenos Aires. Remarkably, the city has produced five top-100 tennis players, but none as successful and beloved as del Potro. Known as "The Tower of Tandil," del Potro stands 6'6" –a relative giant in a sport where mobility is just as important as power. He is the tallest person, along with Marin Čilić, to win a Grand Slam tournament.

Like most Argentinians, his first love was soccer. But one day when he arrived early at soccer practice, a friend gave him a tennis racket to help pass the time. Juan began hitting a ball against a wall and was hooked. He told his parents he wanted to play tennis as well, and he did both until the age of 12 when he decided to go all in on tennis.

Del Potro developed an attacking style of play. Though agile for his size, he knew he wouldn't be able to keep up with guys who were smaller and quicker for very long. So he tried to win points as quickly as possible. His primary weapon was a ferocious forehand that could reach speeds of 110 mph. At his best, he simply overpowered his opponents. After his 2009 U.S. Open triumph, everyone expected del Potro to dominate for the next decade.

Instead, the injury bug bit hard. The first came in 2010 when del Potro started feeling pain in his right wrist. He underwent his first surgery in May of that year. Over the next few years, his left wrist also required three separate surgeries. The operations took a toll on del Potro both physically and mentally. However, by 2018 he had regained his form and rose to a world ranking of No. 3–the highest of his career. That year, he once again made the U.S. Open final, this time losing to Novak Djokovic.

Still just 29 years old, del Potro was ready to reclaim his place among the world's best. Then, during a tournament in 2019, he injured his knee when he slipped near the net. That fall led to four knee surgeries–and the eventual end of a once-promising career. In 2022, del Potro announced his retirement from tennis.

Though injuries ravaged his career, he still accomplished more than most, claiming two Olympic medals, 22 singles titles, and 10 victories over world No. 1 players.

Born: **Sept. 23, 1988**
Hometown: **Tandil, Argentina**
Height: **6'6"**
Plays: **Right**
Turned pro: **2005**
Career best ranking (singles): **3**
   (Aug. 13, 2018)
Grand Slam titles: **1**

Novak Djokovic

Eleven-year-old Novak Djokovic awoke to the sound of explosions and air raid sirens. It was March 24, 1999, and NATO had started a bombing campaign in Belgrade, Yugoslavia, in response to the alleged mistreatment of ethnic Albanians by the country's president Slobodan Milošević. For the next 78 days, Novak would spend nights hunkered down with family and strangers alike in a nearby apartment building's bomb shelter. Above them, F-117 fighter jets dropped their payloads as they roared past.

By that time, Novak already was a known commodity in the tennis world. His father Srdjan was a competitive skier who, along with his wife Dijana, owned a pizza restaurant in the mountain resort town of Kopaonik, where the government had happened to build a tennis complex. Young Novak would linger around the courts until one day Jelena Genčić, who had once coached star Monica Seles, invited him to join her clinic. Within a week, Genčić was singing the praises of this "golden child."

Novak took to tennis instantly. When he was six, he told his parents he wanted to become the top player in the world. The next year, he restated that goal during an interview on Serbian television. Nothing could deter the youngster–not even war. When the bombs started falling, Novak continued his training, practicing up to five hours per day. Genčić would choose practice locations near places that had recently been bombed under the assumption NATO wouldn't target the same sites twice.

If anything, the experience of living in a war zone strengthened Novak's resolve. "These kinds of things make you stronger and hungrier for success, I think, in whatever you choose to do," he said. Shortly after the 11-week campaign ended, Novak set off for Munich, Germany, to attend a tennis academy. He became the top-ranked 14-and-under player in Europe and then the No. 1 16-and-under player. In 2003, he turned pro.

At the time, men's tennis was defined by the great rivalry between Roger Federer and Rafael Nadal. Djokovic wanted to crash their party. He quickly established himself as one of the best serve returners in the game, and he possessed a devastating down-the-line backhand. His first Grand Slam title came at the 2008 Australian Open, where he dispatched Federer in the semifinals before beating Jo-Wilfried Tsonga in the finals.

In 2011, the Big Two officially became the Big Three. Djokovic won his second Australian Open that year by beating Andy Murray. He then lost to Federer in the French Open semis before defeating Nadal in the finals of both Wimbledon and the U.S. Open. Along the way, he grabbed the No. 1 ranking, fulfilling his childhood dream and becoming the first Serb to reach that milestone.

In the years to follow, Djokovic staked a claim for being the best tennis player of all time. He currently owns a men's record of 24 Grand Slam titles, including an unprecedented 10 Australian Open championships. He has won 98 ATP Tour events and has spent an amazing 412 total weeks at No. 1. Federer's 310 total weeks at No. 1 is the mark closest to Djokovic's. At age 37, there is little evidence he is slowing down–though he certainly has nothing left to prove.

Born: **May 22, 1987**

Hometown: **Belgrade, Serbia**

Height: **6'2"**

Plays: **Right**

Turned pro: **2003**

Career best ranking (singles): **1**
   (July 4, 2011)

Grand Slam titles: **24**

Roger Federer

Peter Carter, an Australian tennis coach working at the Old Boys Tennis Club in Basel, Switzerland, saw something special in a student of his named Roger Federer. But he feared the boy's fierce temper would prevent him from reaching his full potential. Hardly a day went by when Roger wouldn't throw his racket against the fence, and during matches he was known to scream "lucky shot" whenever his opponent scored a point against him.

Roger's demeanor was so bad, a coach of his referred to him as "Little Satan." At one tournament, his on-court behavior embarrassed Roger's parents so much they refused to speak to him on the way home. So Carter made it a priority to work on Roger's mental game just as much as his tennis technique. In particular, Carter helped Roger understand just how much energy his outbursts were costing him. Over time, Roger's tantrums came less and less frequently.

However, it took a tragedy for Carter's lessons to fully take hold. In 2002, a 21-year-old Federer was devastated to hear that Carter had been killed in a car crash on his honeymoon in South Africa. The sobering news served as a wake-up call to the budding superstar. He committed himself to becoming the player Carter had always thought he could be. Federer stopped allowing his emotions to control him and developed a clinical coolness on the court. The attitude change unleashed one of the most dominant careers in tennis history.

With a world-class serve and forehand coupled with almost ballet-like movement on the court, Federer took the tennis world by storm in the 2003 Wimbledon tournament when he defeated Mark Philippoussis in straight sets to win his first Grand Slam title. But his reign had just begun. From 2004 through 2007, Federer won 11 out of 16 Grand Slam championships. Only Rafael Nadal's clay court brilliance prevented Federer from taking more. Nadal knocked Federer out of the French Open four consecutive years starting in 2005. Federer finally captured a French Open title in 2009, completing his career Grand Slam.

In February 2004, Federer reached a world ranking of No. 1, and he held it until 2008 when he slid to No. 2 behind Nadal. Nadal's rise–and later Novak Djokovic's–prevented Federer from continuing to completely dominate the sport. However, he still racked up Grand Slams. In 2009, he surpassed Pete Sampras's men's record of 14 career Grand Slam titles with a victory over Andy Roddick at Wimbledon. Then, in 2017, Federer once again bested one of Sampras's records by winning his eighth Wimbledon title. He became the first male player to win 20 Grand Slams when he beat Marin Čilić in the 2018 Australian Open.

By then, injuries and age began to take their toll on Federer. He would make it to only one more Grand Slam final, losing a marathon five-set heartbreaker to Djokovic in the 2019 Wimbledon championship. Federer announced his retirement in 2022 at the age of 41. He won a total of 103 tournaments during his outstanding career. No doubt, he made Coach Carter proud.

Born: **Aug. 8, 1981**

Hometown: **Basel, Switzerland**

Height: **6'1"**

Plays: **Right**

Turned pro: **1998**

Career best ranking (singles): **1** **(Feb. 2, 2004)**

Grand Slam titles: **20**

David Ferrer

When tennis coach Javier Piles had reached the limits of his tolerance with his young pupil's poor work ethic, he literally locked 17-year-old Spaniard David Ferrer in a small, dark storage room and left him there for hours. Ferrer responded to this draconian measure by quitting the game altogether, finding work as a bricklayer instead. He lasted in that grueling job one week before deciding maybe Piles's methods weren't so bad after all.

His lesson learned, the once-lazy boy from Xàbia, Spain, molded himself into one of his sport's hardest workers. At just 5'9" and 160 pounds, Ferrer didn't possess the raw power of many of his peers. As a result, he couldn't rely on a game of ace serves and quick winners. He had to grind for each and every point, relentlessly returning his opponents' shots until they got impatient and made a mistake.

Fittingly, he earned the nickname "Ferru," which means "iron" in Catalan, because of his unyielding spirit. What he lacked in size, he made up for in grit, hand-eye coordination, and athleticism. None other than Roger Federer once called him the best returner in the game, and his defensive style of play took him to great heights. In his 20-year career, he won 27 titles and 734 matches. He was a top-10 player for seven seasons, peaking at No. 3 in the world in 2013.

But even iron has its limits, and Ferrer's limits happened to be named Federer, Nadal, and Djokovic. Against those three, he had a paltry record of 11–59, including going 0–17 against Federer. Unable to find consistent success against the giants of his era, Ferrer ended his career with one glaring blemish on an otherwise impeccable résumé: he never won a Grand Slam title.

Though he once had a stretch beginning with the 2012 Australian Open where he made it to at least the quarterfinals in 10 straight Grand Slam tournaments, he played in just one final: the 2013 French Open. Heading into the championship round, Ferrer hadn't dropped a set all tournament. But waiting for him was fellow countryman Rafael Nadal, the greatest clay court player of all time. Nadal ended Ferrer's dream run in three sets. Ferrer would never again advance past the quarterfinal round in any Grand Slam.

He retired in 2019 at the age of 37 following a second round loss to Alexander Zverev at the Madrid Open. Widely regarded as one of the best players to never win a Grand Slam, by the time his career ended he was also one of the most highly respected players on the tour. Following his loss to Zverev, Ferrer walked to the net amid a standing ovation and placed his headband on the ground. The most tireless worker in tennis could finally take a rest.

Born: **Apr. 2, 1982**

Hometown: **Xàbia, Spain**

Height: **5'9"**

Plays: **Right**

Turned pro: **2000**

Career best ranking (singles): **3 (July 8, 2013)**

Grand Slam titles: **0**

Coco Gauff

The youngest player to ever qualify for Wimbledon couldn't believe it. It was 2019, and Cori Gauff, better known as Coco, had drawn legend Venus Williams in the first round. The 15-year-old from Delray Beach, Florida, grew up idolizing Venus and Serena Williams. Coco even trained on the same public courts at Pompey Park the Williams sisters used for part of their childhood. In fact, Coco's father Corey mapped out a plan for his daughter's tennis career modeled after the one Richard Williams had made for his daughters.

At first, Corey was worried the moment would be too big for his teenager, who, the night before the final qualifying round, was preoccupied with a science test. But Coco was thrilled at the opportunity. She had assumed the Williams sisters would be retired by the time she got on tour.

Coco did more than compete—she defeated Venus in straight sets. Afterward, as the two shook hands at the net, the phenom thanked her idol, telling her she wouldn't be playing tennis without Venus's influence. Then, Gauff kept winning, making it to the round of 16 before losing to eventual champion Simona Halep. And just like that, Gauff was labeled the heir apparent to Venus and Serena.

Her success in that tournament made Gauff a national celebrity, but she had been on the radar in tennis circles for quite some time. At 13, she became the youngest ever to make the finals at the Junior U.S. Open. The next year, she won the Junior French Open and in the process became the youngest junior girl's No. 1 in history.

Coco's athletic prowess didn't come out of nowhere. Corey and Candi Gauff were both Division I athletes themselves. Corey played basketball at Georgia State while Candi ran track and field for Florida State. They saw potential in their daughter from a young age. When she was three, Coco crawled out of her stroller and chased her older cousins around a track with such a look of determination on her face that Candi was certain Coco truly thought she could catch them.

The Gauffs encouraged Coco to try a lot of sports. But gymnastics, soccer, and basketball never spoke to her like tennis did. From the start, Coco displayed an intensity and focus not present in most children. At seven, she would arrive at practice and begin her dynamic warm-up on her own. Already, she could handle more advanced training, such as perfecting the grip of her serve, and she was already talking about one day winning Grand Slam titles.

She reached her first women's Grand Slam final at the age of 18, losing to world No. 1 Iga Świątek. The next year she won the 2023 U.S. Open by defeating Aryna Sabalenka after dropping the first set. At just 19 years old, she realized her childhood dream by becoming a major champion. Odds are, there are many more wins to come.

Born: **Mar. 13, 2004**
Hometown: **Delray Beach, Florida, USA**
Height: **5'9"**
Plays: **Right**
Turned pro: **2018**
Career best ranking:
  Singles: **3 (Sept. 11, 2023)**
  Doubles: **1 (Aug. 15, 2022)**
Grand Slam titles: **1**

Ons Jabeur

Ons Jabeur breaks barriers. The "Trailblazer from Tunisia" is well known for being a woman of firsts. In 2021, she became the first Arab tennis player to break into the world's top 10. The next year, her victory over Jessica Pegula in the Madrid Open marked the first time an Arab or African woman won a Women's Tennis Association 1000-level event. Later that year, Jabeur made history again by becoming the first Arab woman to reach the finals of a Grand Slam event when she took out Germany's Tatjana Maria in the Wimbledon semifinals.

Born August 28, 1994, in Ksar Hellal, Tunisia, Ons was the youngest of four children. Her mother Samira enjoyed playing tennis and frequented the local tennis club to play with her friends. Since Ons was not yet in school, Samira had no choice but to take the three-year-old with her. A self-described troublemaker, Ons couldn't be left alone, so Samira put a racket in her hands and let her play.

By 10, Ons was already dreaming of winning Grand Slams, telling her mother that one day she would be drinking a coffee at Roland-Garros while watching her daughter play in the French Open. At the time, the very thought seemed preposterous. Only one Arab woman had ever cracked the top 100: Selima Sfar peaked at No. 75 in the world in 2001. Early on, Ons would practice on the courts at tourist hotels because tennis clubs in her town of Sousse were scarce. When she divulged her professional aspirations, she was often met with laughter.

But Ons was not so easily deterred. Before she became a teenager, she had already developed a varied game that did not rely solely on power. Instead, she used slices and drop shots to keep her opponents off-balance, earning her the nickname "Roger Federer." She showed enough promise that she moved to the Tunisian capital city of Tunis at 13 to begin training at a multisport academy. At 16 she won the 2011 girls' Junior French Open.

Her transition from junior star to the women's circuit proved difficult. Because Tunisia lacked a tennis culture, Jabeur struggled to put together a competent team to guide her through the early part of her career. Over time, though, she built a strong support system and steadily moved up the rankings, breaking into the top 100 for the first time in 2017 and making her first Grand Slam quarterfinal at the 2020 Australian Open.

She firmly established herself as someone to be reckoned with in 2022, by winning in Madrid. She followed that up by making back-to-back Grand Slam finals in Wimbledon and then the U.S. Open. Though she lost both matches, she finished the year ranked No. 2 in the world behind only Iga Świątek. She demonstrated staying power by again making it to the Wimbledon final in 2023, where she lost to Markéta Vondroušová.

While Jabeur has not captured a Grand Slam title yet, her career can't be considered anything less than a resounding success. A hero in Tunisia —where Jabeur was once honored by having her likeness appear on a commemorative postal stamp—she has inspired millions throughout the Arab world.

Born: **Aug. 28, 1994**

Hometown: **Ksar Hellal, Tunisia**

Height: **5'6"**

Plays: **Right**

Turned pro: **2010**

Career best ranking: (singles): **2 (June 27, 2022)**

Grand Slam titles: **0**

Angelique Kerber

There are tennis prodigies. There are late bloomers. And then there is Angelique Kerber, who took a quarter of a century to reach her apex. Born on January 18, 1988, in Bremen, Germany, to parents of Polish descent, Kerber started playing tennis at the ripe old age of three. She was good enough to turn pro at 15, but for many years afterward she struggled to break through.

Her first big moment came during the 2011 U.S. Open at the age of 23. She entered the tournament ranked No. 92 in the world and had never made it out of the third round in any of her previous 15 Grand Slam appearances. Seemingly out of nowhere, she cruised into the semifinals before losing to Australia's Samantha Stosur.

For the next several seasons, Kerber became a fixture in the top 10, but as the 2016 season started, there was little indication she would ever come close to No. 1. Then, Kerber put together the season of her life.

It started with the Australian Open, the first Grand Slam event of the year. After overcoming match point in the first round, she went on a tear and made her first ever Grand Slam final, where she stunned the tennis world by defeating the great Serena Williams. In doing so, she became the first German to win a major since the legendary Steffi Graf in 1999. Kerber was just getting started. She made the finals at Wimbledon, with Williams avenging her previous loss. She also won a silver medal at the Rio de Janeiro Olympics before capping her year with a U.S. Open championship.

Kerber's performance in the U.S. Open earned her the top ranking. At 28, she became the oldest first-time No. 1 in the history of the sport–by a full three years. So what changed? Kerber has always been known as a defensive player, meaning she likes safe shots and waiting for her opponents to make mistakes. While this style served her fairly well, it meant she had no counters for times when she was being overpowered.

But starting in 2015, she began to play more aggressively, blurring the line between offense and defense. Because her forehand has a short backswing, Kerber can disguise her shot, allowing her either to come around the ball and play sharp angles, slap it flat down the line, or cut a shot short.

With these new wrinkles in her arsenal, Kerber took her game to a whole new level. She proved 2016 was no fluke by defeating Williams again in the 2018 Wimbledon final, claiming her third major championship. She also is proof that, sometimes, you can teach an old tennis player new tricks.

Born: **Jan. 18, 1988**
Hometown: **Bremen, Germany**
Height: **5'8"**
Plays: **Left**
Turned pro: **2003**
Career best ranking (singles): **1**
   (Sept. 12, 2016)
Grand Slam titles: **3**

27

Na Li

Na Li had had enough. It was 2002, and the 20-year-old burgeoning tennis star was tired of having her entire career–her entire life, really–controlled by her country's state-run sports system. So one day, China's No. 1 player packed a small bag of necessities and, without even telling her coaches, left the national training center to attend college in the hopes of becoming a journalist.

Li had never actually wanted to pursue a career in tennis in the first place. That decision was made for her by others. Her father, a former badminton player, enrolled his daughter in a local state-run sports school when she was five years old. It didn't take long, however, for her coaches to conclude that her shoulders and wrists were unsuited to badminton.

Recognizing her athletic ability, however, a coach suggested she try tennis instead. At the time, hardly anybody in China was familiar with the sport, and Na's own parents referred to it merely as "fuzzy ball." Nevertheless, they agreed that Na should pursue this path. By the age of eight, Na was living at the sports school, practicing six days per week in a toxic environment overflowing with criticism. The breaking point came during an awards ceremony in 2001 when the official who placed the third-place medal around Li's neck slapped her. The incident made her decision to quit that much easier.

Li may have given up on China's rigorous sports system, but the system didn't give up on her. In 2003, the head of China's state tennis program, Jinfang Sun, paid Li a visit and encouraged her to come back. She did and, using a rare combination of speed and power, became the first Chinese player to win a Women's Tennis Association title in 2004 as well as cracking the top 25 in 2006.

Still, Li felt stifled by a centralized system that ran every aspect of her career, including who coached her and what tournaments she entered. She even had to give 65 percent of her winnings to the Chinese government. In 2008, Li gave Sun an ultimatum: she would quit for good if not allowed more freedom.

Remarkably, China agreed to let Li have more control. For the first time in her life, Li was allowed to choose her coaches, set her schedule, and keep a higher percentage of her winnings. Her career took off, and on June 4, 2011, 116 million Chinese fans watched her become the first player from an Asian country to win a Grand Slam title when she defeated Francesca Schiavone in the French Open.

Because of Li, who would add the 2014 Australian Open title to her résumé, tennis's popularity in China exploded. She became a national hero–both for her achievements on the court and for her fight for more individual freedom. Because of Li, nobody in China calls tennis "fuzzy ball" anymore.

Born: **Feb. 26, 1982**
Hometown: **Wuhan, China**
Height: **5'8"**
Plays: **Right**
Turned pro: **1999**
Career best ranking (singles): **2**
    (Feb. 17, 2014)
Grand Slam titles: **2**

Daniil Medvedev

Modern men's tennis can at times feel a bit monotonous. For many players, the name of the game is power: powerful serves, powerful forehands, powerful backhands. But Russia's Daniil Medvedev, who entered the 2024 season ranked No. 3 in the world, is different.

The self-described counterattacker is much more than a one-trick pony. His versatile game allows him to evaluate what each individual match requires from him, and he has a seemingly endless bag of tricks from which to pull. He has been described as a "shape-shifter" who takes points where nobody thought they existed and as an "octopus" for his ability to reach balls few others can.

Then again, much about Medvedev's tennis career has been nontraditional. Born in Moscow on February 11, 1996, Daniil's parents signed him up for tennis lessons at the age of six. But unlike some tennis parents who have professional ambitions for their children at a young age, Olga and Sergey Medvedev were only interested in their son's "general development." Aside from tennis, young Daniil also swam, played chess, attended drawing classes, and played soccer.

And while tennis eventually replaced most of his other hobbies, it never was Daniil's sole priority. At an age when a lot of his peers in the tennis world were putting their education on the back burner to focus entirely on their careers, Daniil was enrolled in a prestigious and academically rigorous school. Trying to balance a demanding sport with a demanding education was challenging, but Daniil believed it was important to have a backup plan if tennis didn't pan out.

His failure to fully commit to the sport held him back on the junior circuit. He never went beyond the third round at any major junior tournament. Then, at the relatively late age of 18, he and his parents made the difficult decision to move to France, where he could enroll in the Elite Tennis Center in Cannes.

Finally, tennis had his full attention. Over the next few years, Medvedev's ranking steadily improved, but he had one more opponent to vanquish before his career could really take off: himself. From a young age, Daniil was known for his epic tantrums. On the tennis court, he too often let his emotions get the best of him, costing him countless matches.

Medvedev added a sports psychologist to his team to help him channel his feelings. Additionally, in 2018, he got married. Medvedev credits his wife Daria with helping him control his temper. By 2019, his career had shifted into high gear, as he made his first Grand Slam final, losing to Rafael Nadal in the U.S. Open. Two years later, he defeated Novak Djokovic in that same tournament to claim his first Grand Slam title.

In February 2022, he rose to No. 1 in the world, marking the first time since 2004 that someone other than Djokovic, Nadal, Federer, or Murray held that distinction.

Born: **Feb. 11, 1996**

Hometown: **Moscow, Russia**

Height: **6'6"**

Plays: **Right**

Turned pro: **2014**

Career best ranking (singles): **1**
  (Feb. 28, 2022)

Grand Slam titles: **1**

Andy Murray

Andy Murray rose through the junior tennis ranks alongside peers Rafael Nadal and Novak Djokovic, so there was some understandable frustration–and, yes, envy–during the summer of 2012. Murray had just lost in the Wimbledon final to the great Roger Federer, dropping the Scot's Grand Slam final record to 0–4. Meanwhile, Nadal had already been a major champion 11 times over, and Djokovic had five major titles to his name.

No British man had won one of the Grand Slam tournaments since 1936, and Murray appeared doomed to never break through against the three-headed monster of Federer, Nadal, and Djokovic. Though gifted with speed, power, and a light touch, on the court it seemed as though Murray battled himself as much as his opponent. But then, just like that, everything changed.

Mere weeks after his Wimbledon loss to Federer, Murray found himself on that same court facing that same opponent, this time in the gold medal match of the London Olympics. Finally, Murray defeated Federer. Though it wasn't a Grand Slam win, it felt like a turning point all the same. The next major was the U.S. Open, and Murray made it to the finals again, where Djokovic awaited him. In an epic 4-hour, 54-minute marathon, Murray conquered his demons and came out on top. The Big Three was now the Big Four.

Murray's journey to tennis royalty started in the small town of Dunblane, Scotland, where he grew up in a tennis family. His mother Judy coached the sport and his older brother Jamie is one of the game's top doubles players. Andy demonstrated talent early, but the defining moment of his young career came courtesy of a conversation he had with Nadal at a junior tournament.

Nadal fascinated Murray with a description of his training regimen. The Spaniard said he spent 4.5 hours per day playing tennis outside, practicing against some of the best players in the world. Murray, meanwhile, was maybe playing 4.5 hours per week, primarily with his mother and brother. If he wanted to reach his goals, he realized it meant leaving Dunblane.

So at the age of 15, Murray left his family and moved to Barcelona, where he enrolled at the Sanchez-Casal Academy. There, he regularly practiced with professional players, giving him the opportunity to develop his game with others who took tennis as seriously as he did. The experience also taught him that in order to get where he wanted to go, sometimes difficult decisions had to be made.

Following his breakthrough victory at the 2012 U.S. Open, Murray defeated Djokovic again in the 2013 Wimbledon final for his second Grand Slam title. He added a third in 2016 by winning Wimbledon again over Milos Raonic. With three Grand Slam victories, Murray cemented himself as one of the game's brightest stars.

Born: **May 15, 1987**

Hometown: **Dunblane, Scotland**

Height: **6'3"**

Plays: **Right**

Turned pro: **2005**

Career best ranking (singles): **1**
   (Nov. 7, 2016)

Grand Slam titles: **3**

Rafael Nadal

At 11, Rafael Nadal was forced to choose between his two loves: tennis and soccer. The phenom from the Spanish island of Majorca had just won the Spanish 12-and-under national tennis title, and on the soccer pitch he was a standout left-sided forward. Up until that point, Rafa's soccer coach had allowed him to miss training and still play in games. Then the team got a new coach, who told Rafa that if he wanted to play, he had better participate in all of the team's practices.

Rafa was already devoting four hours per day to tennis, so he realized he couldn't do both sports any longer. Though he was passionate about soccer, that sport for whatever reason always made him anxious in a way tennis never did. So he made the difficult decision to give up soccer and concentrate solely on tennis.

It is, of course, impossible to know how Nadal's soccer career would have unfolded, but it is difficult to believe he would have come close to duplicating what he has accomplished in tennis. Now 38 years old, his 22 Grand Slam titles are second only to Novak Djokovic's 24. And while people can debate whether or not Nadal is the greatest tennis player of all time, he is beyond all doubt the greatest clay court player in history. His 14 French Open titles are eight more than Björn Borg's, whose six victories at Roland-Garros were the pre-Nadal gold standard. At one point in his career, Nadal had won 81 straight matches on clay.

Nadal's path to tennis immortality began at age three. His Uncle Toni, a tennis instructor, one day tossed a ball to his young nephew and was impressed that Rafa moved toward it to hit it instead of doing what most young kids do and waiting for the ball to come to them. Toni kept working with Rafa and eventually became his full-time coach, a position he held until he retired in 2017.

Perhaps nobody had a more prominent role in shaping Nadal's career than Toni. It was he who encouraged Rafa to play left-handed even though Rafa did most things with his right hand. Toni also kept his nephew humble, letting him know it was unacceptable to break his racket when matches didn't go his way. After all, Toni explained, rackets are expensive, and in a world riddled with poverty, Toni expected his pupil to treat his possessions with respect.

Nadal turned pro at 15, and the tenacity with which he played each point quickly endeared him to tennis fans worldwide. He found success while still a teenager, winning his first French Open on his very first try at the age of 19 in 2005. He then proceeded to win the next three. In his first decade of French Open competition, Nadal won the event nine times.

In the meantime, he developed a riveting rivalry with Roger Federer. While Nadal had Federer's number on clay, defeating him in the 2006, 2007, and 2008 French Open finals, Federer had the upper hand on grass, beating Nadal in the Wimbledon final in both 2006 and 2007. But when the two met in the final for a third time in 2008, Nadal finally prevailed, proving he was more than a clay court specialist. Along with his 14 French Open titles, Nadal has won four U.S. Opens, two Wimbledons, and two Australian Opens. It's safe to say Nadal chose wisely when he picked tennis.

Born: **June 3, 1986**
Hometown: **Manacor, Spain**
Height: **6'1"**
Plays: **Left**
Turned pro: **2001**
Career best ranking (singles): **1** **(Aug. 18, 2008)**
Grand Slam titles: **22**

Naomi Osaka

Though it sure didn't look like it, tennis superstar Naomi Osaka of Japan was struggling. It was 2021, and the then 23-year-old had just captured her fourth Grand Slam title by beating Jennifer Brady in straight sets at the Australian Open. As Serena Williams's career wound down, Osaka, who is half Japanese and half Haitian, seemed poised to more than ably fill the legend's sizable shoes and become the next big thing in tennis.

In reality, though, Osaka's career was teetering on the edge. The introverted, socially conscious Osaka had a secret: for years she had battled bouts of depression and often suffered severe anxiety. Things came to a head in the lead-up to the 2021 French Open when Osaka announced she would not speak to the press during the tournament—even though all players are contractually obligated to do so. When she stayed true to her word after her opening round victory, the French Open fined her $15,000.

Osaka responded by withdrawing from the tournament altogether. Soon after, she went public with her mental health issues in announcing her decision to take some time away from tennis. Since then, Osaka—who has been credited with making it less taboo to speak openly about mental health issues—has taken multiple leaves of absence from the game, including all of 2023 while she was pregnant with her first child. As the now 26-year-old strives to return to form, the real question may be how she ever reached the top in the first place.

Naomi Osaka was born on October 16, 1997, in Osaka. When she was a toddler, her parents Leonard François and Tamaki Osaka decided they would take a stab at molding Naomi and her older sister Mari into the next Venus and Serena Williams. This venture eventually led them to New York, where Tamaki worked while Leonard stayed at home to coach the girls. In 2006, Leonard abruptly—and without consulting his wife—pulled his girls out of school, packed up the family van, and moved them to Florida. There, the girls would play tennis during the day and be homeschooled by their father at night.

The lifestyle limited Naomi's contact with other children, helping to explain her discomfort being around people as her career progressed. While Mari's tennis career never took off, Naomi was named the 2016 Newcomer of the Year by the Women's Tennis Association. Her true breakthrough came in 2018 when she stunned Serena Williams in the U.S. Open final to claim her first major. She won her second at the 2019 Australian Open, becoming the first women since Williams in 2015 to win back-to-back majors. That same year, she became the first Asian person to be ranked No. 1.

Osaka added a third Grand Slam to her résumé when she won the 2020 U.S. Open. Whether or not she ever wins a fifth is almost moot. What she has overcome thus far is bigger than tennis, and Osaka deserves to keep her focus on her mental health and well-being.

Born: **Oct. 16, 1997**
Hometown: **Osaka, Japan**
Height: **5'11"**
Plays: **Right**
Turned pro: **2013**
Career best ranking
   (singles): **1**
   (Jan. 28, 2019)
Grand Slam titles: **4**

Jessica Pegula

At first glance, it would seem that the story of Jessica Pegula's tennis career fits the classic underdog tale. Beset with injuries early on, it took Pegula 11 years of being a professional just to crack the top 100. Five years after reaching that hard-fought milestone, Pegula has scratched and clawed her way to a top-5 ranking and holds the distinction of being the top-ranked American tennis player.

On the other hand, most underdogs do not have billionaire parents. Born on February 24, 1994, in Buffalo, New York, Jessica Pegula is the daughter of Terry and Kim Pegula. Terry, having made a fortune in the oil and gas industry, is worth an estimated $6.7 billion and is the principal owner of the National Hockey League's Buffalo Sabres and the National Football League's Buffalo Bills. So Jessica never had to worry about how she would finance her tennis career, and she doesn't need to win to put food on her table.

While having wealth is definitely an advantage in an expensive sport like tennis, forging a successful professional career is a grueling grind for anyone. In other words, money can only take a player so far. In Jessica's case, her tennis journey started at the age of seven, when she became interested in the sport after her older sister Laura took it up. Laura was good enough to play Division I tennis at the University of Pittsburgh.

Jessica Pegula relocated to Florida in 2007 to pursue a tennis career. As a 15-year-old, she worked with Venus and Serena Williams's former hitting coach Dave Rineberg, who was impressed with her explosive power. Shortly after joining with Rineberg, though, Pegula required surgery to remove bone spurs in her right ankle. It wouldn't be the last time she experienced a physical setback. In 2014, a knee injury sidelined her for about 18 months, and then she needed hip surgery in 2017.

By 2021, the "young American" wasn't so young anymore. But, finally healthy, she started seeing results. She made her first Grand Slam quarterfinal at that year's Australian Open, and in 2022 she made the quarterfinal in three of the four Grand Slam tournaments. That year, she also won her first WTA 1000 title in Guadalajara, Mexico. By the end of 2022, the woman who had struggled to crack the top 100 for so long found herself ranked No. 3 in the world.

Though she still hasn't broken through in a Grand Slam, she has maintained a top-5 ranking for a couple of years now. Pegula hardly ever gets beaten by players ranked well below her, meaning she rarely suffers a bad loss. And that level of consistency is something no amount of money can buy.

Born: **Feb. 24, 1994**
Hometown: **Buffalo, New York, USA**
Height: **5'7"**
Plays: **Right**
Turned pro: **2009**
Career best ranking:
    Singles: **3 (Oct. 24, 2022)**
    Doubles: **1 (Sept. 11, 2023)**
Grand Slam titles: **0**

Andrey Rublev

Andrey Rublev doesn't remember how he started playing tennis, but his mother sure does. Marina Marenka recalls watching her then two-year-old crawl past a room full of toys toward a tennis racket and ball sitting in a corner of the room. It was love at first sight.

As he was growing up in Moscow, it was difficult to get Andrey to put his racket down. Sometimes, he would even sleep with it. By the time he was nine or 10, Andrey said he was on the courts from morning until night, eating breakfast, lunch, and dinner between working on his game.

His innate love for sports ran in the family. Marina herself is a tennis coach, and his father Andrey was a professional boxer. On those rare occasions the younger Andrey wasn't on the tennis courts, he could often be found training in a boxing gym. Unlike his father, though, Andrey viewed boxing only as a way to improve his strength and endurance. His passion lay in smashing tennis balls, not faces.

Armed with a monster forehand and a boxer's work ethic, Rublev quickly made a name for himself. In 2013, he won the singles title at the European 16 & Under Championships in his hometown of Moscow. The next year, the offensive baseliner won the Roland-Garros junior championship. As a pro, his breakout year came in 2020, when he earned five singles titles and broke into the top 10 for the first time.

Currently ranked No. 5 in the world, the 26-year-old still hasn't captured that elusive Grand Slam championship, though he has made the quarterfinals 10 times. Off the court, Rublev is known as one of the nicest guys in the sport.

He is also courageous. In February 2022, as Russian president Vladimir Putin prepared to invade Ukraine, Rublev wrote "No War Please" on the glass in front of a camera lens, a gesture all the more risky considering he still has family in Russia.

But on the court, he has been prone to emotional outbursts that detract from his enormous talent. In one now-infamous meltdown in 2023, a frustrated Rublev slammed his racket into his leg repeatedly until his knee became bloody in a match against Carlos Alcaraz.

In an effort to stay centered during stressful matches, Rublev has started to work with a coach with a background in psychology. They practice breathing exercises and energy control while striving to understand when he is most vulnerable to a breakdown. The work may be paying dividends. In the opening round of the 2024 Australian Open, Rublev found himself down 4–1 to Thiago Seyboth Wild in a fifth-set tiebreaker. Rublev kept his cool, rallied, and won the match—a victory in more ways than one.

Born: **Oct. 20, 1997**
Hometown: **Moscow, Russia**
Height: **6'2"**
Plays: **Right**
Turned pro: **2014**
Career best ranking (singles): **5**
   (Sept. 13, 2021)
Grand Slam titles: **0**

Elena Rybakina

Russian-born Elena Rybakina was facing a cross-roads. As she approached high school graduation, the successful junior tennis player had to decide whether to pursue an education—she had been offered scholarships at several U.S. universities—or a professional career in the sport she had been playing since she was six years old.

Tennis wasn't Rybakina's first choice for a sport. As a young child, she also participated in figure skating and gymnastics. But her coaches told her she had no future in those sports because she was too tall. So her father, an avid tennis fan, encouraged his daughter to take up the game he loved so much—and one where her height would be an advantage instead of a hindrance.

Tall, fast, powerful, and graceful, Elena instantly showed promise on the tennis courts. She won the Russian Junior Championships in 2013, and at one point in her junior career she reached No. 3 in the world. Even so, she didn't receive any financial support from Russia, and her parents didn't have the resources needed to finance an aspiring professional tennis player.

So they encouraged their daughter to take the university route. Besides, they worried what Elena would do if she didn't have a college degree and sustained a serious injury. For her part, Elena believed she had what it took to succeed on the court and wanted to prove it; however, without financial assistance she knew she stood little chance.

Then an unexpected door opened. In 2018 the Kazakhstan Tennis Federation offered to provide Rybakina with funding, training, support, and money in exchange for her representing the country. After meeting with KTF president Bulat Utemuratov, Rybakina agreed and became a naturalized Kazakh in July of that year.

Kazakhstan's investment proved a wise one. With proper training and the ability to tour competitively, Rybakina's career blossomed. Standing 6' and known for a blistering serve that can exceed 120 mph and an aggressive style of play, Rybakina's world ranking steadily rose from No. 425 when she first signed the agreement with the KTF to 19th by the end of 2020.

The partnership paid dividends in another way, too. After Russia invaded Ukraine in the winter of 2022, Wimbledon banned all Russian players from competing in that year's tournament. However, since Rybakina was no longer competing for Russia, she was not covered by the ban. Rybakina made the most of it, defeating Simona Halep in the semifinals before overcoming a slow start in the finals against Ons Jabeur to claim the championship. With the victory, the 23-year-old gave Kazakhstan its first-ever Grand Slam title.

She continued her strong play in 2023, reaching the finals of the Australian Open, where she lost to Aryna Sabalenka, and the quarterfinals at Wimbledon. She entered 2024 ranked No. 4 in the world.

Born: **June 17, 1999**
Hometown: **Moscow, Russia**
Height: **6'**
Plays: **Right**
Turned pro: **2014**
Career best ranking (singles): **3** **(June 12, 2023)**
Grand Slam titles: **1**

Aryna Sabalenka

Aryna Sabalenka didn't tell her parents before she got an image of a tiger tattooed on her left forearm when she was 18. When her father saw it, all he could do was laugh. Her mother, on the other hand, refused to talk to her independent daughter for about a week. The temporary silent treatment was worth it, however. With the tattoo serving as an ever-present reminder to fight for every point on the tennis court, the now 26-year-old from Belarus has roared to the apex of the tennis food chain.

With a fiery personality and a powerful game, the 5'11" Sabalenka is known as the "Warrior Princess," and she had a year for the ages in 2023. It began with her first Grand Slam title at the Australian Open and culminated with her wresting the No. 1 world ranking away from Iga Świątek, ending the Pole's 75-week reign at the top of the women's game. She added a second Australian Open title in 2024.

She got her start in tennis somewhat by chance. She recalls her father Sergey, a former hockey player, driving by some tennis courts one day and randomly deciding to stop and introduce his daughter to the game. She took to it immediately.

Sabalenka first made a name for herself in the sport at the 2017 Fed Cup. Belarus entered the tournament without its top-ranked player, Victoria Azarenka, but behind stellar play from Sabalenka, the team reached its first-ever World Group final. Along the way, Sabalenka defeated U.S. Open champion Sloane Stephens, who was ranked No. 13 in the world at the time.

Known as one of tennis's biggest hitters, Sabalenka enjoys pounding the ball from the baseline, and she also employs a powerful serve. At the same time, she isn't afraid to come to the net, either, giving her a well-rounded game that is quite formidable. She combines her raw talent with a feisty personality. Around the age of 12, a family friend called her "a future [Maria] Sharapova." Although it was meant as a compliment, the words infuriated the young competitor. "I'm a future Sabalenka, not a future Sharapova," she shot back.

She locked up the No. 1 ranking during the 2023 U.S. Open when she advanced to the quarter-finals after Świątek was bounced in the previous round. It triggered mixed emotions. For one thing, Sabalenka had hoped she would dethrone her rival on the court, but Świątek's early exit prevented that from happening. For another, it was her father's dream to see his daughter become No. 1 in the world, but Sergey had passed away in 2019 at the age of 43.

Maybe that's why Sabalenka came out flat in the semifinals against Madison Keys, losing the first set 6–0. But Sabalenka displayed her grit and pulled out the next two sets, making her just the third woman in the Open Era to win a Grand Slam semifinal match after failing to win a game in the opening set.

Perhaps the comeback shouldn't be much of a surprise. After all, Sabalenka is a fighter–just ask the tiger on her forearm.

Born: **May 5, 1998**
Hometown: **Minsk, Belarus**
Height: **5'11"**
Plays: **Right**
Turned pro: **2015**
Career best ranking:
   Singles: **1 (Sept. 11, 2023)**
   Doubles: **1 (Feb. 22, 2021)**
Grand slam titles: **2**

Maria Sharapova

Yuri Sharapova moved from Sochi, Russia, to Florida with one purpose in mind: to mold his six-year-old daughter Maria into a world-class tennis champion. Maria first picked up a racket at the age of four, and while taking part in an exhibition in Moscow two years later, she caught the eye of tennis star Martina Navratilova, who encouraged the Sharapovas to relocate to the United States for better training opportunities.

So, leaving his wife Yelena behind and with just $700 in his pocket, Yuri flew to Miami to enroll Maria at Nick Bollettieri's tennis academy, to which Maria had earned a scholarship. Life in their new country was difficult. Neither spoke a word of English, making it hard for Yuri to find work and for Maria to make friends. Maria didn't see her mother for two whole years before Yelena eventually joined them.

Maria trained all day while her father worked several low-wage jobs. They slept on a pullout couch in a tiny apartment owned by a middle-aged Russian woman. Maria learned English from watching TV shows. Feeling like an outsider, she thought the best way to fit in would be to play good tennis—and that she did.

Maria came of age at a time when women's tennis was shifting to a power game, which fit her well. She eventually grew to a height of 6'2", and her game was predicated on a powerful serve and blistering, accurate groundstrokes. According to her, however, her greatest strength was her intense focus. On and off the court, Sharapova was all business. She was not interested in making friends with her competitors, reasoning that doing so would make it more difficult to finish them off.

She turned pro in 2001 at the age of 14 and won her first Grand Slam in 2004 at the age of 17 when she beat Serena Williams in the Wimbledon final. The next year, she reached world No. 1 for the first time, a designation she would hold on five separate occasions in her career. Sharapova would go on to win four more Grand Slams: the 2006 U.S. Open, the 2008 Australian Open, and the 2012 and 2014 French Opens. She is one of just 10 women to win all four Grand Slam tournaments during her career.

In 2016, Sharapova faced a major setback when she tested positive for a banned substance, resulting in a 15-month suspension from the sport. Though she returned to tennis in April 2017, she was plagued by injuries and never regained her form. She announced her retirement from tennis in 2020.

Born: **Apr. 19, 1987**
Hometown: **Nyagan, Russia**
Height: **6'2"**
Plays: **Right**
Turned pro: **2001**
Career best ranking (singles): **1** **(Aug. 22, 2005)**
Grand Slam titles: **5**

Jannik Sinner

Jannik Sinner has conquered mountains, so what does the 23-year-old Italian have to fear on a tennis court? Born in San Candido, a German-speaking town in Northern Italy near the Austrian border, Jannik quite literally grew up on ski slopes, idolizing American skier Bode Miller more than tennis legend Roger Federer. Sinner's parents Hanspeter and Siglinde both worked at a ski lodge, his father as a chef and his mother as a waitress.

And he flashed prodigious talent on skis, winning an Italian championship at age eight and placing second in nationals at 12. At the same time, he enjoyed playing tennis, taking his first swings with a racket at three. Then, at 13, Jannik made the life-altering decision to put aside his skiing pursuits to focus entirely on his tennis game. He left his home and moved to a town called Bordighera near the French border to train at the tennis academy of Riccardo Piatti.

Many factors played a role in Sinner's decision. In skiing, all the training worked up to a 90-second performance where one mistake could cost everything—including your life. In tennis, a player could make multiple mistakes during a match and still find a way to win. In skiing, competitors face the mountain alone and do not know how they have been making out until they cross the finish line. In tennis, the opponent stares at you from straight across the court, and each player knows where he stands at all times.

Though Sinner left competitive skiing behind, his experience with that sport helped him excel at tennis. For one, he displayed a fearlessness on the court, playing near the baseline and hitting not just to return but to win the point. Moreover, just as skiers must keep a near inhuman level of focus for the short time they are zooming down the mountain, tennis players must remain highly focused for the short duration of each point.

At the age of 18 in 2019, Sinner won the ATP Next Gen event for players 21 and younger, and he cracked the top 50 the next year in part by making it to the quarterfinals of the French Open. By 2023 he was ranked No. 4 in the world, but his biggest career accomplishment came at the 2024 Australian Open when he ousted 10-time champion Novak Djokovic in the semifinals before coming back from two sets down to beat Daniil Medvedev in the finals. At just 22, Sinner was a Grand Slam champion.

His decision to stop descending mountains led to his rapid ascent toward tennis's highest peak. Rest assured, Jannik Sinner isn't done climbing yet.

Born: **Aug. 16, 2001**
Hometown: **San Candido, Italy**
Height: **6'2"**
Plays: **Right**
Turned pro: **2018**
Career best ranking (singles): **3**
    (Feb. 19, 2024)
Grand Slam titles: **1**

Iga Świątek

Ambitious athletes often have ambitious dreams. Polish superstar Iga Świątek's dreams, however, were a bit more modest. As a teenager, the extreme introvert would lie in bed wishing only that she could feel more comfortable in social situations. Iga found it difficult to look people in the eye and make small talk. When introduced to somebody new, her mind would go blank.

Luckily for her—and unfortunately for her opponents—tennis is an individual sport, and the 23-year-old winner of four Grand Slam tournaments has already accomplished more in her short career than most players accomplish in their dreams.

To say Poland lacks a rich tennis history is a bit of an understatement. Heading into the 2020 French Open, no Pole had ever won a major tennis championship. Nobody expected that to change anytime soon either. Świątek entered that tournament unseeded and ranked No. 54 in the world. The then 19-year-old finished it as a national hero after she defeated Sofia Kenin in the final in straight sets to make history. Świątek didn't drop a set the entire tournament.

Iga's rise to stardom began in Raszyn, a village outside of Warsaw. Her father Tomasz competed for Poland as a rower at the 1988 Seoul Olympics, and he was the one who pushed Iga and her older sister Agata into sports. In the beginning, tennis was more her father's dream than Iga's. If given the choice, the young girl would have gladly stayed after school playing soccer with her classmates as opposed to going to tennis practice.

Still, her aptitude on the courts was apparent early. At an age when most children find it difficult to return a ball more than once or twice, Iga could hit one against a wall and keep the rally going for dozens and dozens of shots. At practice, she demanded that her coach put her through the same workout as her hardworking sister. Agata was a promising player in her own right before injuries forced her to give up the sport.

Świątek admits she didn't fully embrace tennis until the age of 15 when she played in the Junior French Open and was blown away by the energy of the crowds and the quality of the facilities. Her indoor training facility in Poland didn't even have heat. The experience motivated her to work even harder; Iga Świątek was all in.

By 2022, Świątek's combination of powerful groundstrokes and soft drop volleys had carried her to the No. 2 world ranking behind 25-year-old Australian Ashleigh Barty. Then Barty shocked the tennis world by announcing her retirement, handing the No. 1 ranking to Świątek. As if Świątek felt she had to prove she deserved it, she won two more majors that year: her second French Open and her first U.S. Open. She added a third French Open championship in 2023.

Świątek ended up retaining her No. 1 ranking for 75 straight weeks—the third longest streak in Women's Tennis Association history. Aryna Sabalenka ended Świątek's reign following the 2023 U.S. Open when Świątek bowed out in the round of 16. The greatest Polish tennis player ever may have nothing left to prove, but that's not going to stop her from trying.

Born: **May 31, 2001**

Hometown: **Warsaw, Poland**

Height: **5'9"**

Plays: **Right**

Turned pro: **2016**

Career best ranking (singles): **1**
   (Apr. 4, 2022)

Grand Slam titles: **4**

Dominic Thiem

Doubts consumed Austrian tennis star Dominic Thiem following his five-set loss to Novak Djokovic in the 2020 Australian Open final. The then 26-year-old had long been seen as an heir apparent to the Big Three of Djokovic, Rafael Nadal, and Roger Federer. But following the loss, in which he blew a two to one set lead, Thiem's Grand Slam record fell to 0–3, and he wondered if he would ever fulfill his destiny.

When the COVID-19 pandemic shut the sport down, Thiem was left with little to do but reflect on his career, which, like most professionals, began early. Born in Wiener Neustadt, Austria, in 1993, Dominic first took up the sport at the age of six. Both of his parents—father Wolfgang and mother Karin—were tennis coaches. Wolfgang worked at an academy in Vienna run by Günter Bresnik, a renowned coach who had worked with many top-100 players. Recognizing Dominic's talent, Bresnik himself started coaching the boy when Dominic was just nine.

Dominic's entire family made sacrifices to facilitate his career, with his grandmother even selling her apartment to fund his training. Dominic repaid them with results. By 2011, Thiem was the No. 2 ranked junior player in the world, and he scored his first tour-level win that same year at the Vienna Open. Thiem played the game with astonishing intensity, and he liked to set up far behind the baseline to give himself extra time to connect on his powerful groundstrokes. With a long stroke, his game was perfectly suited for clay, so it was unsurprising that the biggest successes of his early career came at the French Open.

It was in Roland-Garros where he reached his first Grand Slam semifinal, losing to Djokovic in 2016. He broke through in an even bigger way in 2018, reaching the finals before falling to Nadal. The next year, Nadal once again came out on top in the French Open final rematch. So when Thiem came up short once more against one of the Big Three in Australia, it did a number on his psyche.

Then, an unexpected opportunity presented itself. As tennis resumed from its pandemic-induced hiatus in the fall of 2020, neither Federer nor Nadal chose to enter the U.S. Open. Djokovic defaulted in the fourth round after hitting a line judge with a ball he whacked out of anger. With his path clear, Thiem once again found himself in a Grand Slam final, but this time his opponent was German Alexander Zverev, himself vying for his first Grand Slam title.

Perhaps beset by nerves, Thiem dropped the first two sets before storming back, forcing a decisive fifth set, which he won in a tiebreaker. Not only did Thiem finally claim a Grand Slam championship, but he became the first player since 1949 to win a Grand Slam after trailing 2–0 in sets in the final.

Unfortunately, Thiem has struggled to build on that triumph. He injured his wrist the following year and has been unable to return to form thus far. However, still just 30, Thiem's career is far from over.

Born: **Sept. 3, 1993**
Hometown: **Wiener Neustadt, Austria**
Height: **6'1"**
Plays: **Right**
Turned pro: **2011**
Career best ranking (singles): **3 (Mar. 2, 2020)**
Grand Slam titles: **1**

Stefanos Tsitsipas

On a stormy October day in 2016, tennis star Stefanos Tsitsipas nearly lost his life. The then 18-year-old had decided to go for a quick swim with a friend in the choppy waters off Crete, but the two quickly got caught in an undertow and were carried far from shore. In a panic, Tsitsipas furiously tried to swim back, but the harder he fought, the farther out the current took him. Feeling powerless, Tsitsipas began to accept death.

Then, out of nowhere, Tsitsipas's father Apostolos appeared and somehow managed to get his son and his son's friend to safety. The incident changed Tsitsipas's entire outlook. Having stared death in the face and lived, he felt as though there was nothing left to worry about. "I felt fearless, like I could do anything after that," Tsitsipas said.

Now 26 and ranked No. 10 in the world, Tsitsipas is still trying to attack life head-on. On the court, he is known for a blistering forehand, powerful serve, and versatility on each of the sport's surfaces. Off the court, he is an active YouTuber and podcaster, and he also loves to travel and dabbles in photography. For him, it's important to have hobbies to help him detach from tennis sometimes.

Tsitsipas was born in Athens to a family of athletes. His maternal grandfather won a gold medal playing soccer for the Soviet Union in the 1956 Olympics. His mother Julia Salnikova was a former top-200 professional tennis player, and Apostolos both coached and officiated the sport. In fact, the two met while Apostolos was officiating a Women's Tennis Association event in which Salnikova was competing.

Although Greece does not have much of a tennis culture, Tsitsipas began playing when his father put a racket in his hand at age three. By the time he was nine, he had decided he wanted to go all in on tennis. Greece offered him no financial support, so he relied on help from an aunt and other external sources to get his career going.

On the junior circuit, Tsitsipas reached No. 1 in the world, and then he became a household name by upsetting Roger Federer in the fourth round of the 2019 Australian Open on his way to the semifinals. He became the first person from Greece to reach a Grand Slam final at the 2021 French Open, where he fell to Novak Djokovic after winning the first two sets. That year, he climbed to a career-best No. 3 world ranking.

Although he has yet to win a Grand Slam, he's been consistently ranked in the top 10 since 2019. He made a second Grand Slam final in 2023, losing again to Djokovic in the Australian Open. In all, he has made it to at least the semifinals in six Grand Slam tournaments.

Born: **Aug. 12, 1998**
Hometown: **Athens, Greece**
Height: **6'4"**
Plays: **Right**
Turned pro: **2016**
Career best ranking (singles): **3**
    (Aug. 9, 2021)
Grand Slam titles: **0**

Stan Wawrinka

Stan Wawrinka's attempt to grab the tennis spotlight for himself faced one last, albeit imposing, obstacle: world No. 1 player Rafael Nadal. It was the final of the 2014 Australian Open and the first time the nearly 29-year-old Wawrinka had advanced that far in a major. His opponent, meanwhile, already had 13 major titles to his name.

A native of Saint-Barthélemy, Switzerland, Wawrinka had long stood in the shadow of fellow Swiss Roger Federer, who many consider the greatest tennis player of all time. The two countrymen at times even played doubles together, teaming up to win a gold medal at the 2008 Olympics in Beijing. Always, however, Wawrinka was nothing more than "the other guy."

Now, Wawrinka had an opportunity to become just the second Swiss man to win a major championship. To do so, he had to go through Nadal. The two had faced each other a dozen times previously, and Wawrinka had yet to take a single set off the Spaniard. Wawrinka came out strong, displaying the fearless aggression of a man with nothing to lose. He won the first set and was up in the second when Nadal sustained a back injury, limiting his effectiveness. Wawrinka pressed his advantage and claimed the title in a cathartic four-set match.

Finally, Wawrinka was a major champion and a star in his own right.

Wawrinka's journey to the summit of professional tennis had humble beginnings. Saint-Barthélemy is a small town of about 680 residents located some 10 miles from Lausanne and 45 miles from Geneva. His father Wolfram ran a farm that sustained the Centre Social et Curatif, a self-sustaining facility founded to help adults with disabilities develop professional and personal skills to live autonomously.

Born on March 28, 1985, Stan grew up helping his father bale hay and riding in his tractor. His experience with people with special needs helped him learn to fight hard to accomplish what he wanted. In fact, he considered his love for hard work his greatest talent. Stan started playing tennis with his older brother Jonathan at the age of eight. At 15, he quit school to pursue tennis full-time, turning pro at 17 and winning the French Open junior tournament the next year.

Known for his powerful playing style and famous for his devastating one-handed backhand, Wawrinka's Australian Open title vaulted him to the world No. 3 ranking. Afterward, he kept his momentum going, proving his victory over Nadal was no fluke by winning two more majors: the 2015 French Open and the 2016 U.S. Open, each at the expense of Novak Djokovic.

In an era dominated by Federer, Nadal, and Djokovic, Wawrinka and Britain's Andy Murray are the only players outside the Big Three to have won more than two majors since 2004. It's safe to say that Wawrinka now casts a pretty big shadow himself.

Born: **Mar. 28, 1985**

Hometown: **Saint-Barthélemy, Switzerland**

Height: **6'**

Plays: **Right**

Turned pro: **2002**

Career best ranking (singles): **3 (Jan. 27, 2014)**

Grand Slam titles: **3**

Serena Williams

Serena Williams hates losing and always has. Her older half-sister Isha recalls staging family talent shows in her youth where two things were always certain: Serena would sing Whitney Houston's "Greatest Love of All," and Serena would win. Her siblings had learned early on that crowning their baby sister champion was easier than dealing with her tantrums. Good thing, then, that in her professional tennis career, winning came naturally.

Before she had even been born on September 26, 1981, Serena Jameka Williams's father Richard had developed a plan for his children to become tennis stars. The son of a sharecropper in Louisiana, Richard once saw a women's tennis champion awarded a $20,000 check and decided tennis could be the family's ticket to fame and success.

So by the age of three, Serena, along with her older sister Venus, could be found almost daily on the tennis courts, with Richard feeding them ball after ball after ball. Their three older half-sisters played a role in the operation as well, tagging along to pick up the balls until it was time to head home. By then, the Williamses had moved from Michigan to Compton, California, a rough-and-tumble city known more for gang violence than tennis prodigies. This was Richard's conscious decision so that his budding stars would know what could become of them if they failed to work hard and get an education.

For most of Serena's childhood, she lived in the shadow of Venus. From a young age, Venus made the game look easy and Serena idolized her. Serena, being smaller and less powerful at the time than her older sister, had to grind for each victory. But that also helped Serena develop a more well-rounded game incorporating drop shots, great angles, and slices. When she grew bigger, stronger, and more powerful, winning came all the more easily.

Most tennis experts had assumed Venus would win a Grand Slam before her younger sister, but it was Serena who broke through first, winning the 1999 U.S. Open at the age of 17. She was the first Black woman to win a major in the Open Era. In 2002, Serena fully asserted her dominance, not just over Venus but the entire sport. Starting with that year's French Open, Serena would win four straight Grand Slams, culminating in the 2003 Australian Open. Her opponent in all four finals? Venus Williams.

The 2002 season ended with Serena and Venus ranked No. 1 and No. 2, respectively, in the world. Richard's preposterous decades-old vision had come to fruition: His daughters undeniably ruled the world of tennis. Serena would maintain dominance for the next 20 years. By the time she retired in 2022, she had won 23 Grand Slam titles, the most ever by a woman in the Open Era. But more than that, she helped revolutionize—and modernize—the women's game. She ushered in a period defined by power and athleticism while inspiring millions of Black girls across the country.

Born: **Sept. 26, 1981**

Hometown: **Compton, California, USA**

Height: **5'9"**

Plays: **Right**

Turned pro: **1995**

Career best ranking:
   Singles: **1**
   (July 8, 2002)
   Doubles: **1**
   (June 7, 2010)

Grand Slam titles: **23**

Venus Williams

The most consequential tournament in women's tennis history just may have been the 1978 French Open. During that competition, a man named Richard Williams watched Romanian tennis player Virginia Ruzici receive $20,000 for winning the final, and he decided then and there that his children, as yet unborn, would become tennis stars. He wrote up a 78-page plan to make this dream a reality. Then, on June 17, 1980, Richard's wife Oracene gave birth to a daughter. They named her Venus, and Richard set his plan in motion.

Venus Ebony Starr Williams developed her tennis game on the public courts in Compton, California, a working-class city that at the time had a median income for a family of four at just $13,000. It was a far cry from the country clubs and tennis academies where most future tennis professionals learn to play. Even so, Richard diligently drove his daughter to the courts and fed her ball after ball after ball. Eventually, he quit his job as a security guard to coach Venus—and her younger sister Serena—full-time.

From a young age, Venus's prodigious athletic ability was quite evident. Before deciding to focus on tennis, Venus was a track star who once ran a 5:29 mile—at the age of eight. When she was 10 years old, *Sports Illustrated* published a feature-length article on her. By then, she was one of the top players in Southern California, and many considered her the future of tennis. Already nearly six feet tall, Venus demonstrated a blend of size and speed that the women's game just hadn't seen before.

All the while, Richard insisted on guiding her in his own way. He made the decision to pull Venus from the junior circuit to avoid the intense pressure there, and he insisted she stay in school and get good grades. Still, the Williamses briefly moved to Florida to train with famed coach Rick Macci. But after a couple of years they returned to California and Richard resumed coaching duties.

Williams made her professional debut in 1994 at age 14. Three years later, she became the first unseeded U.S. Open women's finalist in the Open Era before losing to Martina Hingis. She fulfilled her destiny in 2000 when she won both Wimbledon and the U.S. Open, and she successfully defended both of those titles the next year. In 2002, she became the first Black tennis player to capture the No. 1 world ranking.

Though a seven-time Grand Slam champion (she won Wimbledon three more times, in 2005, 2007, and 2008), her legacy extends far beyond titles and trophies. She blazed a trail for future Black players, including her sister Serena. Williams's power came from being secure in her identity. As a teenager in 1997, she told reporters, "I'm tall. I'm Black. Everything's different about me. Just face the facts."

She also used her influence to persuade Wimbledon to pay female players as much as their male counterparts. She voiced objections to the gender pay gap in 2005 and drew attention to the matter further by writing an op-ed in the *London Times* in 2006. When Williams won the event in 2007, her paycheck finally matched that of the men's champion. In more ways than one, Venus Williams forever changed the game of women's tennis.

Born: **June 17, 1980**

Hometown: **Compton, California, USA**

Height: **6'1"**

Plays: **Right**

Turned Pro: **1994**

Career best ranking:

Singles: **1** **(Feb. 25, 2002)**

Doubles: **1** **(June 7, 2010)**

Grand Slam titles: **7**

M. BERRETTINI
4R   3-6,6-3,6-3,6-3

2:57
WARM-UP

July 16, 2023, London, England: Carlos Alcaraz and Novak Djokovic go toe to toe in the men's final at Wimbledon.